THE SECRET OF GETTING AHEAD IS GETTING STARTED.

MARK TWAIN

THIS JOURNAL BELONGS TO:

....

Setting goals is the first step in turning the invisible into the visible.

Tony Robbins

TODAY IS: .... / .... / ....

TODAY I AM MOST GRATEFUL FOR

1..
....
2..
....
3..
....

GREAT MOMENTS

....
....
....
....
....

HAPPINESS TRACKER

♡   ♡   ♡   ♡   ♡

TODAY IS: ..../......./............

TODAY I AM MOST GRATEFUL FOR

1..

....

2..

....

3..

....

GREAT MOMENTS

....

....

....

....

....

HAPPINESS TRACKER

♡   ♡   ♡   ♡   ♡

TODAY IS: .... / .... / ....

TODAY I AM MOST GRATEFUL FOR

1...
....
2...
....
3...
....

GREAT MOMENTS

....
....
....
....
....

HAPPINESS TRACKER

♡ ♡ ♡ ♡ ♡

TODAY IS: .... / .... / ....

TODAY I AM MOST GRATEFUL FOR

1...
....
2...
....
3...
....

GREAT MOMENTS

....
....
....
....
....

HAPPINESS TRACKER

♡   ♡   ♡   ♡   ♡

TODAY IS: ..../......./...........

TODAY I AM MOST GRATEFUL FOR

1...
....
2...
....
3...
....

GREAT MOMENTS

....
....
....
....
....

HAPPINESS TRACKER

♡ ♡ ♡ ♡ ♡

TODAY IS: .... / .... / ....

TODAY I AM MOST GRATEFUL FOR

1..
....
2..
....
3..
....

GREAT MOMENTS

....
....
....
....
....

HAPPINESS TRACKER

♡   ♡   ♡   ♡   ♡

TODAY IS: ..../......./............

TODAY I AM MOST GRATEFUL FOR

1..
....
2..
....
3..
....

GREAT MOMENTS

....
....
....
....
....

HAPPINESS TRACKER

♡   ♡   ♡   ♡   ♡

Only I can change my life. No one can do it for me.

Carol Burnett

TODAY IS: .... / .... / ....

TODAY I AM MOST GRATEFUL FOR

1. ....
....
2. ....
....
3. ....
....

GREAT MOMENTS

....
....
....
....
....

HAPPINESS TRACKER

♡   ♡   ♡   ♡   ♡

TODAY IS: ..../......./...........

TODAY I AM MOST GRATEFUL FOR

1..
....
2..
....
3..
....

GREAT MOMENTS

....
....
....
....
....

HAPPINESS TRACKER

♡ ♡ ♡ ♡ ♡

TODAY IS: .... / .... / ....

TODAY I AM MOST GRATEFUL FOR

1. ....
....
2. ....
....
3. ....
....

GREAT MOMENTS

....
....
....
....
....

HAPPINESS TRACKER

♡ ♡ ♡ ♡ ♡

TODAY IS: ..../......./............

TODAY I AM MOST GRATEFUL FOR

1...
....
2...
....
3...
....

GREAT MOMENTS

....
....
....
....
....

HAPPINESS TRACKER

♡   ♡   ♡   ♡   ♡

TODAY IS: .... / .... / ....

TODAY I AM MOST GRATEFUL FOR

1..

2..

3..

GREAT MOMENTS

....

....

....

....

....

HAPPINESS TRACKER

♡   ♡   ♡   ♡   ♡

TODAY IS: .... / .... / ....

TODAY I AM MOST GRATEFUL FOR

1. ....
....
2. ....
....
3. ....
....

GREAT Moments

....
....
....
....
....

HAPPINESS TRACKER

♡   ♡   ♡   ♡   ♡

TODAY IS: ..../......./............

TODAY I AM MOST GRATEFUL FOR

1..
....
2..
....
3..
....

GREAT MOMENTS

....
....
....
....
....

HAPPINESS TRACKER

♡   ♡   ♡   ♡   ♡

Optimism is the faith that leads to achievement. Nothing can be done without hope and confidence.

Helen Keller

TODAY IS: .... / .... / ....

TODAY I AM MOST GRATEFUL FOR

1...
....
2...
....
3...
....

GREAT MOMENTS

....
....
....
....
....

HAPPINESS TRACKER

♡   ♡   ♡   ♡   ♡

TODAY IS: ..../......./............

TODAY I AM MOST GRATEFUL FOR

1...
....
2...
....
3...
....

GREAT MOMENTS

....
....
....
....
....

HAPPINESS TRACKER

♡   ♡   ♡   ♡   ♡

TODAY IS: .... / .... / ....

TODAY I AM MOST GRATEFUL FOR

1. ....
....
2. ....
....
3. ....
....

GREAT MOMENTS

....
....
....
....
....

HAPPINESS TRACKER

♡   ♡   ♡   ♡   ♡

TODAY IS: .... / .... / ....

TODAY I AM MOST GRATEFUL FOR

1. ....
....
2. ....
....
3. ....
....

GREAT MOMENTS

....
....
....
....
....

HAPPINESS TRACKER

♡　♡　♡　♡　♡

TODAY IS: .... / .... / ....

TODAY I AM MOST GRATEFUL FOR

1. ....
....
2. ....
....
3. ....
....

GREAT MOMENTS

....
....
....
....
....

HAPPINESS TRACKER

♡ ♡ ♡ ♡ ♡

TODAY IS: ..../......./............

TODAY I AM MOST GRATEFUL FOR

1...
....
2...
....
3...
....

GREAT MOMENTS

....
....
....
....
....

HAPPINESS TRACKER

♡   ♡   ♡   ♡   ♡

TODAY IS: .... / .... / ....

TODAY I AM MOST GRATEFUL FOR

1..
....
2..
....
3..
....

GREAT MOMENTS

....
....
....
....
....

HAPPINESS TRACKER

If you fell down yesterday, stand up today.

H. G. Wells

TODAY IS: .... / .... / ....

TODAY I AM MOST GRATEFUL FOR

1. ....
....
2. ....
....
3. ....
....

GREAT MOMENTS

....
....
....
....
....

HAPPINESS TRACKER

♡   ♡   ♡   ♡   ♡

TODAY IS: .... / .... / ....

TODAY I AM MOST GRATEFUL FOR

1..
....
2..
....
3..
....

GREAT MOMENTS

....
....
....
....
....

HAPPINESS TRACKER

♡ ♡ ♡ ♡ ♡

TODAY IS: ……. / ……. / …………

TODAY I AM MOST GRATEFUL FOR

1. ……………………………………………………………………………………
……………………………………………………………………………………
2. ……………………………………………………………………………………
……………………………………………………………………………………
3. ……………………………………………………………………………………
……………………………………………………………………………………

GREAT MOMENTS

……………………………………………………………………………………
……………………………………………………………………………………
……………………………………………………………………………………
……………………………………………………………………………………
……………………………………………………………………………………

HAPPINESS TRACKER

♡ ♡ ♡ ♡ ♡

TODAY IS: ..../......./............

TODAY I AM MOST GRATEFUL FOR

1...
....
2...
....
3...
....

GREAT MOMENTS

....
....
....
....
....

HAPPINESS TRACKER

♡ ♡ ♡ ♡ ♡

TODAY IS: .... / .... / ....

TODAY I AM MOST GRATEFUL FOR

1. ....

....

2. ....

....

3. ....

....

GREAT MOMENTS

....

....

....

....

....

HAPPINESS TRACKER

♡ ♡ ♡ ♡ ♡

TODAY IS: .... / .... / ....

TODAY I AM MOST GRATEFUL FOR

1..
....
2..
....
3..
....

GREAT MOMENTS

....
....
....
....
....

HAPPINESS TRACKER

♡ ♡ ♡ ♡ ♡

TODAY IS: .... / .... / ....

TODAY I AM MOST GRATEFUL FOR

1..

....

2..

....

3..

....

GREAT MOMENTS

....

....

....

....

....

HAPPINESS TRACKER

♡ ♡ ♡ ♡ ♡

Keep your eyes on the stars, and your feet on the ground.

Theodore Roosevelt

TODAY IS: .... / .... / ....

TODAY I AM MOST GRATEFUL FOR

1..
....
2..
....
3..
....

GREAT MOMENTS

....
....
....
....
....

HAPPINESS TRACKER

♡ ♡ ♡ ♡ ♡

TODAY IS: ..../......./............

TODAY I AM MOST GRATEFUL FOR

1..
....
2..
....
3..
....

GREAT MOMENTS

....
....
....
....
....

HAPPINESS TRACKER

♡   ♡   ♡   ♡   ♡

TODAY IS: ..../......./............

TODAY I AM MOST GRATEFUL FOR

1..
....
2..
....
3..
....

GREAT MOMENTS

....
....
....
....
....

HAPPINESS TRACKER

♡　　♡　　♡　　♡　　♡

TODAY IS: ..../......./............

TODAY I AM MOST GRATEFUL FOR

1..
....
2..
....
3..
....

GREAT MOMENTS

....
....
....
....
....

HAPPINESS TRACKER

♡   ♡   ♡   ♡   ♡

TODAY IS: ..../......./............

TODAY I AM MOST GRATEFUL FOR

1...
....
2...
....
3...
....

GREAT MOMENTS

....
....
....
....
....

HAPPINESS TRACKER

♡　♡　♡　♡　♡

TODAY IS: ..../......./............

TODAY I AM MOST GRATEFUL FOR

1...
....
2...
....
3...
....

GREAT MOMENTS

....
....
....
....
....

HAPPINESS TRACKER

♡   ♡   ♡   ♡   ♡

TODAY IS: .... / .... / ....

TODAY I AM MOST GRATEFUL FOR

1. ....
....
2. ....
....
3. ....
....

GREAT MOMENTS

....
....
....
....
....

HAPPINESS TRACKER

♡ ♡ ♡ ♡ ♡

The most effective way to do it, is to do it.

Amelia Earhart

TODAY IS: .... / .... / ....

TODAY I AM MOST GRATEFUL FOR

1. ....
....
2. ....
....
3. ....
....

GREAT MOMENTS

....
....
....
....
....

HAPPINESS TRACKER

♡ ♡ ♡ ♡ ♡

TODAY IS: .... / .... / ....

TODAY I AM MOST GRATEFUL FOR

1...
....
2...
....
3...
....

GREAT MOMENTS

....
....
....
....
....

HAPPINESS TRACKER

TODAY IS: .... / .... / ....

TODAY I AM MOST GRATEFUL FOR

1..

....

2..

....

3..

....

GREAT MOMENTS

....

....

....

....

....

HAPPINESS TRACKER

♡   ♡   ♡   ♡   ♡

TODAY IS: .... / .... / ....

TODAY I AM MOST GRATEFUL FOR

1...
....
2...
....
3...
....

GREAT MOMENTS

....
....
....
....
....

HAPPINESS TRACKER

♡   ♡   ♡   ♡   ♡

TODAY IS: ..../......./............

TODAY I AM MOST GRATEFUL FOR

1...
....
2...
....
3...
....

GREAT MOMENTS

....
....
....
....
....

HAPPINESS TRACKER

♡　　♡　　♡　　♡　　♡

TODAY IS: ..../......./............

TODAY I AM MOST GRATEFUL FOR

1...
....
2...
....
3...
....

GREAT MOMENTS

....
....
....
....
....

HAPPINESS TRACKER

TODAY IS: .... / .... / ....

TODAY I AM MOST GRATEFUL FOR

1. ....
....
2. ....
....
3. ....
....

GREAT MOMENTS

....
....
....
....
....

HAPPINESS TRACKER

♡   ♡   ♡   ♡   ♡

Life is 10% what happens to you and 90% how you react to it.

Charles R. Swindoll

TODAY IS: .... / .... / ....

TODAY I AM MOST GRATEFUL FOR

1..

....

2..

....

3..

....

GREAT MOMENTS

....

....

....

....

....

HAPPINESS TRACKER

♡   ♡   ♡   ♡   ♡

TODAY IS: .... / .... / ....

TODAY I AM MOST GRATEFUL FOR

1...
....
2...
....
3...
....

GREAT MOMENTS

....
....
....
....
....

HAPPINESS TRACKER

♡　　♡　　♡　　♡　　♡

TODAY IS: .... / .... / ....

TODAY I AM MOST GRATEFUL FOR

1..
....
2..
....
3..
....

GREAT MOMENTS

....
....
....
....
....

HAPPINESS TRACKER

♡ ♡ ♡ ♡ ♡

TODAY IS: ...... / ...... / ....

TODAY I AM MOST GRATEFUL FOR

1..
....
2..
....
3..
....

GREAT MOMENTS

....
....
....
....
....

HAPPINESS TRACKER

♡   ♡   ♡   ♡   ♡

TODAY IS: .... / .... / ....

TODAY I AM MOST GRATEFUL FOR

1...
....
2...
....
3...
....

GREAT MOMENTS

....
....
....
....
....

HAPPINESS TRACKER

♡ ♡ ♡ ♡ ♡

TODAY IS: ..../......./............

TODAY I AM MOST GRATEFUL FOR

1..

2..

3..

GREAT MOMENTS

....

....

....

....

....

HAPPINESS TRACKER

♡ ♡ ♡ ♡ ♡

TODAY IS: .... / .... / ....

TODAY I AM MOST GRATEFUL FOR

1...
....
2...
....
3...
....

GREAT MOMENTS

....
....
....
....
....

HAPPINESS TRACKER

♡   ♡   ♡   ♡   ♡

A CREATIVE MAN IS MOTIVATED
BY THE DESIRE TO ACHIEVE,
NOT BY THE DESIRE TO BEAT OTHERS.

AYN RAND

TODAY IS: ..../......./............

TODAY I AM MOST GRATEFUL FOR

1...
....
2...
....
3...
....

GREAT MOMENTS

....
....
....
....
....

HAPPINESS TRACKER

♡   ♡   ♡   ♡   ♡

TODAY IS: ..../......./............

TODAY I AM MOST GRATEFUL FOR

1...
....
2...
....
3...
....

GREAT MOMENTS

....
....
....
....
....

HAPPINESS TRACKER

♡   ♡   ♡   ♡   ♡

TODAY IS: ..../......./............

TODAY I AM MOST GRATEFUL FOR

1..

....

2..

....

3..

....

GREAT MOMENTS

....

....

....

....

....

HAPPINESS TRACKER

♡ ♡ ♡ ♡ ♡

TODAY IS: .... / .... / ....

TODAY I AM MOST GRATEFUL FOR

1...
....
2...
....
3...
....

GREAT MOMENTS

....
....
....
....
....

HAPPINESS TRACKER

♡ ♡ ♡ ♡ ♡

TODAY IS: .... / .... / ....

TODAY I AM MOST GRATEFUL FOR

1..
....
2..
....
3..
....

GREAT MOMENTS

....
....
....
....
....

HAPPINESS TRACKER

♡   ♡   ♡   ♡   ♡

TODAY IS: .... / .... / ....

TODAY I AM MOST GRATEFUL FOR

1. ....
....
2. ....
....
3. ....
....

GREAT MOMENTS

....
....
....
....
....

HAPPINESS TRACKER

♡ ♡ ♡ ♡ ♡

TODAY IS: ..../......./.............

TODAY I AM MOST GRATEFUL FOR

1..
....
2..
....
3..
....

GREAT MOMENTS

....
....
....
....
....

HAPPINESS TRACKER

♡   ♡   ♡   ♡   ♡

A GOAL IS A DREAM WITH A DEADLINE.

Napoleon Hill

TODAY IS: ...... / ...... / ....

TODAY I AM MOST GRATEFUL FOR

1. ....
....
2. ....
....
3. ....
....

GREAT MOMENTS

....
....
....
....
....

HAPPINESS TRACKER

♡   ♡   ♡   ♡   ♡

TODAY IS: ..../......./............

TODAY I AM MOST GRATEFUL FOR

1..
....
2..
....
3..
....

GREAT Moments

....
....
....
....
....

HAPPINESS TRACKER

♡ ♡ ♡ ♡ ♡

TODAY IS: ..../......./............

TODAY I AM MOST GRATEFUL FOR

1..
....
2..
....
3..
....

GREAT MOMENTS

....
....
....
....
....

HAPPINESS TRACKER

♡ ♡ ♡ ♡ ♡

TODAY IS: ..../......./............

TODAY I AM MOST GRATEFUL FOR

1..
....
2..
....
3..
....

GREAT MOMENTS

....
....
....
....
....

HAPPINESS TRACKER

♡ ♡ ♡ ♡ ♡

TODAY IS: .... / .... / ....

TODAY I AM MOST GRATEFUL FOR

1...
....
2...
....
3...
....

GREAT MOMENTS

....
....
....
....
....

HAPPINESS TRACKER

♡　　♡　　♡　　♡　　♡

TODAY IS: ..../......./............

TODAY I AM MOST GRATEFUL FOR

1..
....
2..
....
3..
....

GREAT MOMENTS

....
....
....
....
....

HAPPINESS TRACKER

♡   ♡   ♡   ♡   ♡

TODAY IS: .... / .... / ....

TODAY I AM MOST GRATEFUL FOR

1..
....
2..
....
3..
....

GREAT MOMENTS

....
....
....
....
....

HAPPINESS TRACKER

♡   ♡   ♡   ♡   ♡

WE AIM ABOVE THE MARK
TO HIT THE MARK.

Ralph Waldo Emerson

TODAY IS: .... / .... / ....

TODAY I AM MOST GRATEFUL FOR

1...
....
2...
....
3...
....

GREAT MOMENTS

....
....
....
....
....

HAPPINESS TRACKER

♡   ♡   ♡   ♡   ♡

TODAY IS: .... / .... / ....

TODAY I AM MOST GRATEFUL FOR

1..
....
2..
....
3..
....

GREAT MOMENTS

....
....
....
....
....

HAPPINESS TRACKER

♡   ♡   ♡   ♡   ♡

TODAY IS: .... / .... / ....

TODAY I AM MOST GRATEFUL FOR

1..
....
2..
....
3..
....

GREAT MOMENTS

....
....
....
....
....

HAPPINESS TRACKER

♡ ♡ ♡ ♡ ♡

TODAY IS: ..../......./...........

TODAY I AM MOST GRATEFUL FOR

1..
....
2..
....
3..
....

GREAT MOMENTS

....
....
....
....
....

HAPPINESS TRACKER

♡   ♡   ♡   ♡   ♡

TODAY IS: ..../......./............

TODAY I AM MOST GRATEFUL FOR

1...

....

2...

....

3...

....

GREAT MOMENTS

....

....

....

....

....

HAPPINESS TRACKER

♡ ♡ ♡ ♡ ♡

TODAY IS: ..../......./...........

TODAY I AM MOST GRATEFUL FOR

1...
....
2...
....
3...
....

GREAT MOMENTS

....
....
....
....
....

HAPPINESS TRACKER

♡   ♡   ♡   ♡   ♡

TODAY IS: .... / .... / ....

TODAY I AM MOST GRATEFUL FOR

1...
....
2...
....
3...
....

GREAT MOMENTS

....
....
....
....
....

HAPPINESS TRACKER

♡   ♡   ♡   ♡   ♡

BE KIND WHENEVER POSSIBLE.
IT IS ALWAYS POSSIBLE.

DALAI LAMA

TODAY IS: ..../......./............

TODAY I AM MOST GRATEFUL FOR

1...
....
2...
....
3...
....

GREAT MOMENTS

....
....
....
....
....

HAPPINESS TRACKER

♡ ♡ ♡ ♡ ♡

TODAY IS: ..../......./............

TODAY I AM MOST GRATEFUL FOR

1..
....
2..
....
3..
....

GREAT MOMENTS

....
....
....
....
....

HAPPINESS TRACKER

♡ ♡ ♡ ♡ ♡

TODAY IS: ..../......./............

TODAY I AM MOST GRATEFUL FOR

1...
....
2...
....
3...
....

GREAT MOMENTS

....
....
....
....
....

HAPPINESS TRACKER

♡   ♡   ♡   ♡   ♡

TODAY IS: .... / .... / ....

TODAY I AM MOST GRATEFUL FOR

1...
....
2...
....
3...
....

GREAT MOMENTS

....
....
....
....
....

HAPPINESS TRACKER

♡ ♡ ♡ ♡ ♡

TODAY IS: .... / .... / ....

TODAY I AM MOST GRATEFUL FOR

1...
....
2...
....
3...
....

GREAT MOMENTS

....
....
....
....
....

HAPPINESS TRACKER

♡ ♡ ♡ ♡ ♡

TODAY IS: ..../......./............

TODAY I AM MOST GRATEFUL FOR

1...
....
2...
....
3...
....

GREAT MOMENTS

....
....
....
....
....

HAPPINESS TRACKER

♡   ♡   ♡   ♡   ♡

TODAY IS: .... / .... / ....

TODAY I AM MOST GRATEFUL FOR

1. ....
....
2. ....
....
3. ....
....

GREAT MOMENTS

....
....
....
....
....

HAPPINESS TRACKER

♡   ♡   ♡   ♡   ♡

IF YOU CAN DREAM IT,
YOU CAN DO IT.

WALT DISNEY

TODAY IS: ..../......./............

TODAY I AM MOST GRATEFUL FOR

1...
....
2...
....
3...
....

GREAT MOMENTS

....
....
....
....
....

HAPPINESS TRACKER

♡ ♡ ♡ ♡ ♡

TODAY IS: ..../......./............

TODAY I AM MOST GRATEFUL FOR

1..
....
2..
....
3..
....

GREAT MOMENTS

....
....
....
....
....

HAPPINESS TRACKER

♡ ♡ ♡ ♡ ♡

TODAY IS: .... / .... / ....

TODAY I AM MOST GRATEFUL FOR

1..
....
2..
....
3..
....

GREAT MOMENTS

....
....
....
....
....

HAPPINESS TRACKER

TODAY IS: ..../......./.............

TODAY I AM MOST GRATEFUL FOR

1..
....
2..
....
3..
....

GREAT MOMENTS

....
....
....
....
....

HAPPINESS TRACKER

♡ ♡ ♡ ♡ ♡

TODAY IS: ..../......./............

TODAY I AM MOST GRATEFUL FOR

1..
....
2..
....
3..
....

GREAT MOMENTS

....
....
....
....
....

HAPPINESS TRACKER

♡   ♡   ♡   ♡   ♡

TODAY IS: .... / .... / ....

TODAY I AM MOST GRATEFUL FOR

1. ....
   ....
2. ....
   ....
3. ....
   ....

GREAT MOMENTS

....
....
....
....
....

HAPPINESS TRACKER

♡ ♡ ♡ ♡ ♡

TODAY IS: .... / .... / ....

TODAY I AM MOST GRATEFUL FOR

1. ....
....
2. ....
....
3. ....
....

GREAT MOMENTS

....
....
....
....
....

HAPPINESS TRACKER

♡ ♡ ♡ ♡ ♡

PROBLEMS ARE NOT STOP SIGNS, THEY ARE GUIDELINES.

Robert H. Schuller

TODAY IS: .... / .... / ....

TODAY I AM MOST GRATEFUL FOR

1...

....

2...

....

3...

....

GREAT MOMENTS

....

....

....

....

....

HAPPINESS TRACKER

♡ ♡ ♡ ♡ ♡

TODAY IS: .... / .... / ....

TODAY I AM MOST GRATEFUL FOR

1..

....

2..

....

3..

....

GREAT MOMENTS

....

....

....

....

....

HAPPINESS TRACKER

♡ ♡ ♡ ♡ ♡

TODAY IS: .... / .... / ....

TODAY I AM MOST GRATEFUL FOR

1..
....
2..
....
3..
....

GREAT MOMENTS

....
....
....
....
....

HAPPINESS TRACKER

♡   ♡   ♡   ♡   ♡

TODAY IS: .... / .... / ....

TODAY I AM MOST GRATEFUL FOR

1...
....
2...
....
3...
....

GREAT MOMENTS

....
....
....
....
....

HAPPINESS TRACKER

♡ ♡ ♡ ♡ ♡

TODAY IS: .... / .... / ....

TODAY I AM MOST GRATEFUL FOR

1..

....

2..

....

3..

....

GREAT MOMENTS

....

....

....

....

....

HAPPINESS TRACKER

♡   ♡   ♡   ♡   ♡

TODAY IS: ..../......./............

TODAY I AM MOST GRATEFUL FOR

1...
....
2...
....
3...
....

GREAT MOMENTS

....
....
....
....
....

HAPPINESS TRACKER

♡　　♡　　♡　　♡　　♡

TODAY IS: .... / .... / ....

TODAY I AM MOST GRATEFUL FOR

1. ....

....

2. ....

....

3. ....

....

GREAT MOMENTS

....

....

....

....

....

HAPPINESS TRACKER

♡   ♡   ♡   ♡   ♡

If you don't like how things are, change it! You're not a tree.

Jim Rohn

TODAY IS: .... / .... / ....

TODAY I AM MOST GRATEFUL FOR

1. ....
....
2. ....
....
3. ....
....

GREAT MOMENTS

....
....
....
....
....

HAPPINESS TRACKER

♡   ♡   ♡   ♡   ♡

TODAY IS: ..../......./............

TODAY I AM MOST GRATEFUL FOR

1..
....
2..
....
3..
....

GREAT MOMENTS

....
....
....
....
....

HAPPINESS TRACKER

TODAY IS: ...... / ...... / ....

TODAY I AM MOST GRATEFUL FOR

1...
....
2...
....
3...
....

GREAT MOMENTS

....
....
....
....
....

HAPPINESS TRACKER

♡ ♡ ♡ ♡ ♡

TODAY IS: ..../......./............

TODAY I AM MOST GRATEFUL FOR

1...
....
2...
....
3...
....

GREAT MOMENTS

....
....
....
....
....

HAPPINESS TRACKER

♡ ♡ ♡ ♡ ♡

TODAY IS: .... / .... / ....

TODAY I AM MOST GRATEFUL FOR

1. ....

....

2. ....

....

3. ....

....

GREAT MOMENTS

....

....

....

....

....

HAPPINESS TRACKER

♡   ♡   ♡   ♡   ♡

TODAY IS: .... / .... / ....

TODAY I AM MOST GRATEFUL FOR

1. ....
....
2. ....
....
3. ....
....

GREAT MOMENTS

....
....
....
....
....

HAPPINESS TRACKER

♡ ♡ ♡ ♡ ♡

TODAY IS: .... / .... / ....

TODAY I AM MOST GRATEFUL FOR

1. ....
....
2. ....
....
3. ....
....

GREAT MOMENTS

....
....
....
....
....

HAPPINESS TRACKER

♡　　♡　　♡　　♡　　♡

You don't get paid for the hour. You get paid for the value you bring to the hour.

Jim Rohn

TODAY IS: .... / .... / ....

TODAY I AM MOST GRATEFUL FOR

1..
....
2..
....
3..
....

GREAT MOMENTS

....
....
....
....
....

HAPPINESS TRACKER

♡   ♡   ♡   ♡   ♡

TODAY IS: ..../......./............

TODAY I AM MOST GRATEFUL FOR

1..
....
2..
....
3..
....

GREAT MOMENTS

....
....
....
....
....

HAPPINESS TRACKER

♡ ♡ ♡ ♡ ♡

TODAY IS: ..../......./............

TODAY I AM MOST GRATEFUL FOR

1...
....
2...
....
3...
....

GREAT MOMENTS

....
....
....
....
....

HAPPINESS TRACKER

♡ ♡ ♡ ♡ ♡

TODAY IS: .... / .... / ....

TODAY I AM MOST GRATEFUL FOR

1..
....
2..
....
3..
....

GREAT MOMENTS

....
....
....
....
....

HAPPINESS TRACKER

♡   ♡   ♡   ♡   ♡

TODAY IS: .... / .... / ....

TODAY I AM MOST GRATEFUL FOR

1..
....
2..
....
3..
....

GREAT MOMENTS

....
....
....
....
....

HAPPINESS TRACKER

♡   ♡   ♡   ♡   ♡

TODAY IS: .... / .... / ....

TODAY I AM MOST GRATEFUL FOR

1...
....
2...
....
3...
....

GREAT MOMENTS

....
....
....
....
....

HAPPINESS TRACKER

♡   ♡   ♡   ♡   ♡

TODAY IS: .... / .... / ....

TODAY I AM MOST GRATEFUL FOR

1...
....
2...
....
3...
....

GREAT MOMENTS

....
....
....
....
....

HAPPINESS TRACKER

♡   ♡   ♡   ♡   ♡

It does not matter how slowly you go as long as you do not stop.

Confucius

TODAY IS: .... / .... / ....

TODAY I AM MOST GRATEFUL FOR

1...
....
2...
....
3...
....

GREAT MOMENTS

....
....
....
....
....

HAPPINESS TRACKER

♡   ♡   ♡   ♡   ♡

TODAY IS: ..../......../.............

TODAY I AM MOST GRATEFUL FOR

1..
....
2..
....
3..
....

GREAT MOMENTS

....
....
....
....
....

HAPPINESS TRACKER

TODAY IS: .... / .... / ....

TODAY I AM MOST GRATEFUL FOR

1...
....
2...
....
3...
....

GREAT MOMENTS

....
....
....
....
....

HAPPINESS TRACKER

♡　　♡　　♡　　♡　　♡

TODAY IS: ..../......./............

TODAY I AM MOST GRATEFUL FOR

1...
....
2...
....
3...
....

GREAT MOMENTS

....
....
....
....
....

HAPPINESS TRACKER

♡　　♡　　♡　　♡　　♡

TODAY IS: ..../......./............

TODAY I AM MOST GRATEFUL FOR

1..
....
2..
....
3..
....

GREAT MOMENTS

....
....
....
....
....

HAPPINESS TRACKER

♡ ♡ ♡ ♡ ♡

TODAY IS: .... / .... / ....

TODAY I AM MOST GRATEFUL FOR

1...
....
2...
....
3...
....

GREAT MOMENTS

....
....
....
....
....

HAPPINESS TRACKER

♡ ♡ ♡ ♡ ♡

TODAY IS: .... /........ /..............

TODAY I AM MOST GRATEFUL FOR

1...
....
2...
....
3...
....

GREAT MOMENTS

....
....
....
....
....

HAPPINESS TRACKER

♡   ♡   ♡   ♡   ♡

WITH THE NEW DAY COMES NEW STRENGTH AND NEW THOUGHTS.

ELEANOR ROOSEVELT

TODAY IS: ..../......./............

TODAY I AM MOST GRATEFUL FOR

1...
....
2...
....
3...
....

GREAT MOMENTS

....
....
....
....
....

HAPPINESS TRACKER

♡   ♡   ♡   ♡   ♡

TODAY IS: ……. / ……. / …………

TODAY I AM MOST GRATEFUL FOR

1……………………………………………………………………………………
………………………………………………………………………………………
2……………………………………………………………………………………
………………………………………………………………………………………
3……………………………………………………………………………………
………………………………………………………………………………………

GREAT MOMENTS

………………………………………………………………………………………
………………………………………………………………………………………
………………………………………………………………………………………
………………………………………………………………………………………
………………………………………………………………………………………

HAPPINESS TRACKER

TODAY IS: .... / .... / ....

TODAY I AM MOST GRATEFUL FOR

1..

....

2..

....

3..

....

GREAT MOMENTS

....

....

....

....

....

HAPPINESS TRACKER

♡ ♡ ♡ ♡ ♡

TODAY IS: ..../......./...........

TODAY I AM MOST GRATEFUL FOR

1..
....
2..
....
3..
....

GREAT MOMENTS

....
....
....
....
....

HAPPINESS TRACKER

♡   ♡   ♡   ♡   ♡

TODAY IS: ..../......./...........

TODAY I AM MOST GRATEFUL FOR

1..
....
2..
....
3..
....

GREAT MOMENTS

....
....
....
....
....

HAPPINESS TRACKER

♡　♡　♡　♡　♡

TODAY IS: ..../......./............

TODAY I AM MOST GRATEFUL FOR

1...
....
2...
....
3...
....

GREAT MOMENTS

....
....
....
....
....

HAPPINESS TRACKER

♡   ♡   ♡   ♡   ♡

TODAY IS: .... / .... / ....

TODAY I AM MOST GRATEFUL FOR

1...
....
2...
....
3...
....

GREAT MOMENTS

....
....
....
....
....

HAPPINESS TRACKER

♡   ♡   ♡   ♡   ♡

MY NOTES

MY NOTES

....

....

....

....

....

....

....

....

....

....

....

....

....

....

....

....

....

....

....

www.phoenix7.eu

CPSIA information can be obtained
at www.ICGtesting.com
Printed in the USA
LVHW082313240122
709297LV00027B/684